# DOES COLOUR AFFECT MOOD?

Shrijo

**Shrijo Publications**

# INTRODUCTION

Colour, an integral part of our visual experience, has the power to evoke emotions, influence perceptions, and shape our mood. The relationship between colour and mood is a fascinating subject that has intrigued researchers, artists, and psychologists alike. From the calming hues of blue to the energetic vibrancy of red, each colour possesses a unique psychological impact on individuals. This book aims to delve into the intricate connection between colour and mood, exploring how different colours can elicit varied emotional responses.

## The Psychological Influence of Colours

Colours have been found to have a profound impact on human psychology. Warm colours, such as reds and yellows, are often associated with energy, warmth, and stimulation. In contrast, cool colours, like blues and greens, tend to evoke feelings of calmness, tranquillity, and serenity. Understanding the psychological underpinnings of each colour can provide insights into how they influence our emotional state.

## Cultural and Personal Variations

It's essential to acknowledge that the impact of colour on mood is not universally consistent. Cultural backgrounds, personal experiences, and individual preferences play a significant role in shaping how colours are perceived. For example, in Western cultures, white is often associated with purity and weddings, while in some Eastern cultures, it may symbolize mourning. Similarly, personal experiences with specific colours can lead to unique emotional associations.

## Blue: The Calming Hue

Blue is renowned for its calming effects. It is often linked to feelings of serenity, peace, and stability. Studies have suggested that exposure to the colour blue can lower blood pressure and reduce stress levels. Consequently, blue is frequently used in healthcare settings to create a soothing environment.

## Red: The Colour of Passion and Energy

On the other end of the spectrum, red is a colour that elicits strong emotional responses. It is associated with passion, energy, and excitement. Red can raise the heart rate and stimulate adrenaline production, making it a powerful colour for creating a sense of urgency or intensity.

## *Yellow: The Optimistic Hue*

Yellow is often associated with positivity, happiness, and optimism. It can evoke feelings of warmth and joy. However, excessive exposure to bright yellow may lead to feelings of agitation, highlighting the delicate balance required in utilizing colour to achieve a specific mood.

## *Green: Nature's Tranquilizer*

Green, being associated with nature, growth, and renewal, has a tranquilizing effect. It is often used to create spaces that promote relaxation and balance. The colour green has been linked to reduced anxiety and improved mood, making it a popular choice for environments where a sense of harmony is desired.

In conclusion, the relationship between colour and mood is a complex interplay of psychological, cultural, and personal factors. The colours that surround us can significantly impact our emotions, influencing everything from our stress levels to our overall sense of well-being.

Whether we seek the calming embrace of blues, the passionate energy of reds, or the optimistic glow of yellows, understanding the psychological nuances of colour allows us to harness its power to shape our moods and enhance our daily experiences.

As we continue to explore the fascinating realm of colour psychology, we unveil the potential to create environments that not only please the eye but also nurture our emotional well-being.

# THE PSYCHOLOGICAL INFLUENCE OF COLOURS

Colours, beyond their visual aesthetics, possess a profound psychological influence on human emotions and behaviour. The study of colour psychology delves into the intricate ways in which different hues can impact our mood, perceptions, and even physiological responses.

This book aims to explore the fascinating realm of the psychological influence of colours, shedding light on how our minds interpret and respond to the vibrant spectrum that surrounds us.

## *Warm Colours: Energetic and Stimulating*

Warm colours, such as reds, oranges, and yellows, are known for their energetic and stimulating effects. Red, in particular, is associated with passion and intensity, eliciting strong emotional responses. These colours have been linked to increased heart rate and heightened alertness, making them suitable for environments that require energy and attention, such as sports arenas or promotional materials.

## *Cool Colours: Calming and Serene*

On the opposite end of the spectrum, cool colours like blues and greens tend to have calming and serene effects. Blue, often associated with the sky and the ocean, is known for promoting a sense of tranquillity and reducing stress. Hospitals and healthcare settings frequently use cool colours to create a soothing atmosphere conducive to healing and relaxation.

## *Yellow: The Colour of Optimism*

Yellow is the colour of sunshine and is often associated with positivity, happiness, and optimism. It can evoke feelings of warmth and joy, making it a popular choice for spaces where a lively and uplifting atmosphere is desired. Yellow is believed to stimulate mental activity and enhance creativity, making it a favourable colour in educational settings.

## *Green: Nature's Harmony*

Green, as the colour of nature, represents growth, harmony, and balance. Exposure to green environments has been linked to reduced stress and increased feelings of well-being. Incorporating green into interior spaces or urban design can create a connection with nature, fostering a sense of calm and rejuvenation.

## Purple: Regal and Mystical

Purple is often associated with royalty, luxury, and a sense of mystery. It combines the energy of red with the calming properties of blue, making it a colour that can evoke a range of emotions. Purple is often used in marketing to convey a sense of elegance and sophistication.

## Neutral Colours: Versatility and Sophistication

Neutral colours, such as black, white, and gray, are known for their versatility and sophistication. Black is associated with power and elegance, while white symbolizes purity and simplicity. These colours can be used to create a timeless and classic aesthetic, allowing other colours to stand out or providing a clean backdrop for various design elements.

In conclusion, the psychological influence of colours is a dynamic and multifaceted aspect of human perception. From the energetic warmth of reds to the calming serenity of blues, each colour carries its own set of psychological associations.

Designers, marketers, and individuals alike can leverage the power of colour to evoke specific emotions, create atmospheres, and influence behaviour. As we continue to unravel the intricate interplay between colour and psychology, we gain valuable insights into how the hues that surround us shape our experiences and contribute to the rich tapestry of human emotions.

# CULTURAL AND PERSONAL VARIATIONS

The dynamic interplay between colours and mood is a complex terrain influenced not only by psychological factors but also by cultural backgrounds and personal experiences. Understanding how colours impact mood and how these effects vary across cultures and individuals adds depth to the exploration of colour psychology.

This book seeks to delve into the intricate relationship between cultural and personal variations in colours and mood, emphasizing the diverse ways in which individuals and societies perceive and respond to the emotional palette.

## *Cultural Significance in Colour-Mood Associations*

Cultural backgrounds shape the meanings attributed to colours and their impact on mood. For instance, the colour red, symbolizing luck and prosperity in Chinese culture, can evoke feelings of excitement and positivity. In contrast, Western cultures may associate red with passion and energy. The cultural lens through which colours are viewed extends to their ability to influence emotional states, contributing to a kaleidoscope of colour-mood associations.

## Cultural Symbolism and Emotional Resonance

Cultural symbolism extends beyond mere aesthetic preferences; it deeply influences emotional resonance with colours. The calming effect of blue may be heightened in cultures where blue is associated with tranquillity and spirituality. Conversely, cultures with vibrant colour traditions may find intense hues invigorating rather than overwhelming, altering the emotional impact of colours on mood.

## Personal Experiences and Emotional Connections

Personal experiences serve as a unique filter through which individuals perceive and react to colours. A colour that symbolizes joy for one person might evoke melancholy for another due to distinct life experiences. Personal memories, cultural traditions, and upbringing all contribute to the emotional association's individuals form with colours, making the link between colour and mood highly individualized.

## Individual Preferences and Emotional Comfort

Individual preferences in colour choices not only reflect personal taste but also impact emotional comfort. A person drawn to earthy tones may find solace and calmness in these colours, creating a personalized sanctuary. These preferences, influenced by personality traits and mood disorders, contribute to the emotional resonance that colours hold for individuals.

## Cultural Influences in Therapeutic Environments

The impact of colours on mood extends to therapeutic practices, with cultural considerations playing a significant role. While Western psychological theories may emphasize the calming effects of cool colours, other cultures may leverage vibrant and warm colours in therapeutic settings. Understanding the cultural nuances allows for more effective and culturally sensitive therapeutic interventions.

## Synthesis of Cultural and Personal Variations:

The synthesis of cultural and personal variations forms a unique psychosocial tapestry of colour-mood associations. While cultural backgrounds provide a broad framework, personal experiences weave intricate patterns, shaping the emotional impact of colours on an individual level.

This synthesis contributes to the richness and diversity of emotional responses to colours across different societies and individuals.

In conclusion, the interaction between colours and mood in psychology is not a universal phenomenon but a nuanced exploration of cultural and personal variations. As we navigate the intricate landscape of colour psychology, it becomes evident that cultural backgrounds and personal experiences paint the emotional canvas with diverse hues.

Acknowledging and appreciating these variations enhance our understanding of the intricate relationship between colours and mood, fostering a more inclusive and comprehensive perspective on the impact of colours on the human psyche.

# BLUE: THE CALMING HUE

Blue, with its tranquil aura reminiscent of the sky and ocean, stands out as a colour with a remarkable ability to influence human mood. Explored through the lens of colour psychology, the calming properties of blue have been widely recognized and utilized across various domains. This book aims to delve into the psychological aspects of how the colour blue influences mood, providing insights into its therapeutic potential and the diverse ways in which it shapes our emotional experiences.

## Associations with Nature

The calming effects of blue can be attributed, in part, to its association with nature. The vast expanse of the sky and the serene depths of the ocean evoke feelings of openness, tranquillity, and stability. When exposed to the colour blue, individuals often experience a sense of calm reminiscent of natural landscapes, promoting relaxation and emotional equilibrium.

## Physiological Responses

Studies in colour psychology have revealed that exposure to the colour blue can induce physiological responses conducive to a relaxed state. It has been observed to lower blood pressure, heart rate, and even reduce feelings of anxiety. This physiological calming effect makes blue a preferred choice for creating environments that aim to alleviate stress and promote overall well-being.

## Cultural Symbolism

Beyond its physiological impact, the calming influence of blue is also culturally ingrained. In many cultures, blue is associated with stability, trustworthiness, and reliability. The colour is often used in professional settings to convey a sense of competence and reliability, reinforcing positive associations with the colour in various aspects of life.

## Therapeutic Applications

The calming properties of blue find practical applications in therapeutic settings. Mental health professionals often leverage the colour blue in therapy rooms to create a soothing atmosphere. Its ability to induce a sense of calmness can aid in reducing anxiety and stress, contributing to a conducive environment for emotional exploration and healing.

## Blue in Design and Architecture

Designers and architects recognize the impact of colour on mood, and blue is frequently employed in spaces designed for relaxation and reflection. From bedrooms to meditation rooms, the calming hue of blue fosters a sense of serenity, making it a popular choice for creating environments that promote restful sleep and mental tranquillity.

## Blue as a Counterbalance

In the realm of colour psychology, blue is often used as a counterbalance to more energetic and stimulating colours. When combined with warmer tones, blue can temper the intensity, creating a harmonious and balanced visual experience. This duality allows blue to play a versatile role in influencing mood based on its context and surrounding colours.

In conclusion, the calming properties of the colour blue represent a fascinating exploration within the realm of colour psychology. From its association with nature to its physiological impact and cultural symbolism, blue emerges as a versatile and soothing hue.

Whether applied in therapeutic settings, design choices, or cultural representations, the calming influence of blue transcends mere aesthetics, leaving an indelible mark on our emotional experiences. As we continue to unravel the psychology of mood and colour, the calming embrace of blue remains a steadfast and compelling subject for exploration and application in various facets of our lives.

# RED: THE COLOUR OF PASSION AND ENERGY

In the rich tapestry of colour psychology, red emerges as a vibrant and dynamic hue, evoking strong emotional responses associated with passion and energy. This book seeks to unravel the intricate interplay between the colour red and human mood, exploring the psychological dimensions that make red a compelling force in shaping our emotions and influencing our experiences.

*Biological Stimulus*

The colour red has been recognized as a potent biological stimulus that triggers heightened physiological responses. Research indicates that exposure to the colour red can increase heart rate, raise blood pressure, and stimulate adrenaline production. These physiological reactions contribute to the perception of red as an intense and energizing colour.

## Symbolism of Passion

Red has long been symbolically linked to passion and love across diverse cultures. The deep, intense hue of red is associated with the fervour of emotions, making it a powerful symbol of love, desire, and romantic intensity. In art, literature, and cultural traditions, red often serves as an embodiment of passionate expression.

## Energetic and Attention-Grabbing

Red's inherent vibrancy and boldness make it a colour that naturally commands attention. In the realm of design and marketing, red is strategically employed to create visual impact and stimulate interest. Its energetic qualities make it effective in grabbing attention, whether in advertising, signage, or product packaging.

## Cultural Variations in Symbolism

While red universally symbolizes passion, the specific cultural connotations can vary. In Eastern cultures, red is often associated with good luck, prosperity, and celebration, frequently seen in auspicious events and traditional attire. Understanding these cultural variations adds depth to the emotional associations tied to the colour red.

## Impact on Mood and Behaviour

The psychological impact of red on mood extends beyond the immediate physiological responses. Studies suggest that exposure to red can evoke a sense of urgency and influence behaviour, contributing to increased motivation and a willingness to take risks. In this way, red becomes a colour that not only signifies passion but also prompts action.

## Red in Context

The mood-altering effects of red are context-dependent. While it exudes passion and energy, excessive use of red or its misuse in certain contexts can lead to feelings of overwhelm or agitation. Understanding the delicate balance in incorporating red in various environments is crucial to harnessing its positive emotional impact.

In conclusion, red stands as a captivating colour in the realm of colour psychology, wielding the power to stir emotions, ignite passion, and energize the human spirit. From its biological effects on the body to its cultural symbolism and impact on behaviour, red transcends mere visual appeal, becoming a dynamic force that shapes our mood and influences our experiences.

As we continue to explore the intricate relationship between colour and emotion, red stands out as a vivid and compelling chapter, adding depth and intensity to the emotional palette of the human psyche.

# YELLOW: THE OPTIMISTIC HUE

In the vast spectrum of colour psychology, yellow emerges as a radiant and optimistic hue, capable of evoking feelings of joy, warmth, and positivity.

This book endeavours to delve into the psychological dimensions of the colour yellow and its profound impact on human mood. From its association with sunshine to its uplifting qualities, yellow stands as a vibrant force in shaping our emotional experiences.

## Association with Sunlight and Positivity

Yellow's natural association with sunlight positions it as a colour linked to warmth and positivity. Just as the sun brightens the day, the colour yellow has the power to illuminate our emotional landscape, fostering a sense of optimism and well-being. The visual connection to sunlight creates an immediate and positive impact on mood.

## *Symbolism of Joy and Happiness*

Culturally and symbolically, yellow is often associated with joy, happiness, and energy. It is a colour that exudes a sense of light-heartedness and cheerfulness. In various traditions, yellow flowers, such as sunflowers, are gifted to convey positive sentiments and celebrate joyous occasions.

## *Stimulating Mental Activity*

Yellow is known to stimulate mental activity and enhance cognitive processes. Exposure to the colour yellow is believed to increase alertness and creativity, making it an optimal choice for environments where mental engagement and innovation are desired. Its ability to promote intellectual energy contributes to its optimistic psychological impact.

## *Energizing and Uplifting*

Yellow's vibrant and energizing qualities contribute to its uplifting effect on mood. Whether used in interior design, clothing, or art, yellow has the power to infuse spaces with a sense of vitality and enthusiasm. Its presence can counteract feelings of lethargy and instil a positive, dynamic atmosphere.

## *Cultural Variations in Symbolism*

While universally associated with positivity, the specific cultural symbolism of yellow can vary. In some cultures, yellow may represent wealth and prosperity, while in others, it may carry religious or spiritual significance. Understanding these cultural variations enriches our appreciation of the diverse emotional associations tied to the colour yellow.

## *Caution and Overstimulation*

While yellow is predominantly associated with optimism, it is important to note its potential for overstimulation. In excess, yellow can be overwhelming and may contribute to feelings of anxiety or restlessness. Striking a balance in the use of yellow is key to harnessing its positive impact without inducing discomfort.

In conclusion, yellow stands as a beacon of optimism in the realm of colour psychology, radiating positivity and warmth. From its symbolic association with joy to its stimulating effects on mental activity, yellow plays a crucial role in shaping our emotional experiences.

As we continue to explore the intricate relationship between colour and mood, the optimistic hue of yellow remains a compelling and uplifting chapter, inviting us to bask in its vibrant glow and embrace the positive energy it imparts to our lives.

# GREEN: NATURE'S TRANQUILIZER

Amid the vibrant palette of colours, green stands out as a hue with a unique and calming influence on human mood. Often referred to as "nature's tranquilizer," green is intricately tied to the natural world and has the power to evoke feelings of serenity, balance, and tranquillity.

This book aims to delve into the psychology of mood in relation to the colour green, exploring how its association with nature contributes to its calming effects on the human psyche.

## *Natural Association with Nature*

Green, being the colour prevalent in lush landscapes, symbolizes nature, growth, and renewal. The human connection to nature is deeply rooted, and exposure to the colour green taps into an innate sense of tranquillity. Whether it's the verdant foliage of trees or the expansive meadows, green invokes a calming and grounding experience reminiscent of the outdoors.

## *Calming Physiological Responses*

Studies in colour psychology suggest that exposure to green can lead to physiological responses associated with relaxation. Green has been shown to lower stress levels, reduce muscle tension, and create a sense of calmness. Its gentle and harmonious wavelength contributes to a soothing impact on the nervous system.

## *Symbolism of Balance and Harmony*

Green is often associated with balance and harmony due to its prevalence in the natural world. The balance of warm and cool tones in green creates a visual equilibrium that translates into a sense of calm. In design and art, green is strategically used to instil a harmonious and balanced aesthetic, contributing to a peaceful atmosphere.

## *Therapeutic Applications:*

Recognizing the calming influence of green, it is frequently utilized in therapeutic settings. Hospitals, clinics, and mental health facilities often incorporate shades of green to create a healing environment. The colour's association with nature promotes a sense of tranquillity that can aid in reducing anxiety and stress during therapeutic interventions.

## *Elevating Mood and Well-being*

Green has been linked to improved mood and enhanced well-being. Exposure to green spaces, whether in the form of parks, gardens, or natural landscapes, has been associated with increased feelings of happiness and relaxation. The colour's ability to evoke positive emotions contributes to its role as a mood-enhancing element.

## *Cultural Symbolism*

Across cultures, green holds positive symbolism. In many societies, it represents luck, fertility, and prosperity. The positive cultural associations further contribute to green's reputation as a colour that promotes feelings of calmness and positive well-being.

In conclusion, green emerges as a powerful and natural tranquilizer within the realm of colour psychology. Its association with nature, calming physiological responses, and symbolic representation of balance contribute to its profound impact on human mood.

As we navigate the intricate relationship between colour and emotion, green remains a soothing and invigorating presence, inviting individuals to immerse themselves in the tranquil embrace of nature's calming hue.

# CONCLUSION

In the exploration of the question, "Does colour affect mood?" the diverse and intricate relationship between colour and human emotion becomes increasingly evident. Colours are not mere visual stimuli but powerful communicators that influence our psychological state and shape our experiences.

The kaleidoscope of hues, each with its unique psychological footprint, contributes to the rich tapestry of our emotional lives.

As we navigate this colourful journey, it is essential to acknowledge the nuanced interplay of biological, psychological, cultural, and personal factors in determining how colours impact mood. From the calming blues to the passionate reds, the optimistic yellows to the tranquil greens, each colour weaves a narrative that extends beyond aesthetics into the realms of emotion, culture, and individuality.

In the broader context, understanding the influence of colour on mood holds relevance in various fields – from design and marketing to healthcare and psychology. It empowers us to create environments that align with our emotional intentions, fostering well-being, productivity, and positive experiences.

As we continue to explore the captivating intersection of colour and mood, let it serve as a reminder of the dynamic and ever-evolving nature of our perceptual world. The colours that surround us are not just hues on a palette; they are agents of emotion, conveying messages that transcend language and resonate with the very essence of our humanity.

# ABOUT THE AUTHOR

## Shrijo

Shrijo is an Indian Author. She is a Writer, Poetess, Youtuber, Mentor and an Orator.

She writes books about ADHD, Developmental Delay, Depression, Anxiety, Anger Management, Debt Management, Ketogenic Diet, Memory Improvement, Motivation, Education Books, Parenting, Special Education, Psychology, Health Care, and so on. Her books available in Amazon, Scribd, Pustaka, Storytel etc.,